Autumn

Name _____

September
At-Home Activities

Parents, please post this chart at home.
Check off activities as you complete them.

Week 1

☐ Read a book together. Ask your child to retell the story.

☐ Ask your child to count the doors in your house.

☐ Hop around the yard together, first on two feet and then on one foot.

☐ Read a book together. Ask your child to tell you about his or her favorite part.

Week 2

☐ Have your child match the pairs of socks in the laundry.

☐ Take a "listening walk" around the neighborhood. See how many different sounds your child can hear (traffic, people, animals, etc.).

Week 3

☐ Read a book together. Ask your child to name the characters in the story.

☐ Help your child name the pieces of furniture in your living room.

☐ Have your child count out the forks and spoons needed to set the table for dinner.

Week 4

☐ Read a book together. Ask your child to act out something that happened in the story.

☐ Play "I Spy" using color and shape clues: "I spy something red. It is round." (answer: a ball)

☐ Play a board game or a card game together as a family.

Seasonal Activities • EMC 2002 • © Evan-Moor Corp.

Name _____

October
At-Home Activities

Parents, please post this chart at home.
Check off activities as you complete them.

Week 1

☐ Read a book together. Ask your child to identify where the story takes place.

☐ Encourage your child to count to 20 (higher if possible). Give help when needed.

☐ Make a healthy snack together. Talk about the ingredients and tools you use.

Week 2

☐ Read a book together. Ask your child to tell you his or her favorite part.

☐ Ask your child to name the objects and equipment in the bathroom.

☐ Go for a "color hunt." Select one color. Have your child find and name objects in that color around the house and yard.

Week 3

☐ Read a book together. Ask your child to act out something that happened in the story.

☐ Play catch with a softball or a beanbag.

☐ Play the "echo" game. You say a word; your child repeats it. Then you say two words. Your child repeats them. Continue adding one word at a time as long as your child can successfully repeat them.

Week 4

☐ Read a book together. Ask, "Did you like this story? Why?"

☐ Help your child find objects around the house and yard that begin with the same sound as *bee*.

☐ Play a board game or a card game together as a family.

Name _____

November
At-Home Activities

Parents, please post this chart at home.
Check off activities as you complete them.

Week 1

☐ Read a book together. Ask your child to retell the story.

☐ Ask your child to count pennies. Put the pennies in sets of five and explain that five pennies are the same amount as one nickel.

☐ Skip around the yard with your child. (Some children find this difficult. Be patient and keep trying.)

Week 2

☐ Read a book together. Ask your child to tell you about his or her favorite part.

☐ Have your child help fold the towels in the laundry. Talk together about the feel, smell, and color of the freshly washed towels.

☐ Take a "touching walk." Touch objects with different textures—tree bark, smooth leaves, etc.

Week 3

☐ Read a book together. Ask your child to name the characters in the story.

☐ Help your child name objects and tools in the kitchen.

☐ Help your child practice kicking a ball.

Week 4

☐ Read a book together. Ask your child to act out something that happened in the story.

☐ Play the "rhyming game." Say two words. Your child decides if the words rhyme: "bell, tell" "Yes, they rhyme"; "bell, top" "No, they don't rhyme."

☐ Play a board game or a card game together as a family.

Name _____

Autumn Leaves

Color the picture.

Autumn is here!
The leaves are falling.

Trace the letters.   autumn

Name _____

Falling Leaves

Color the picture.

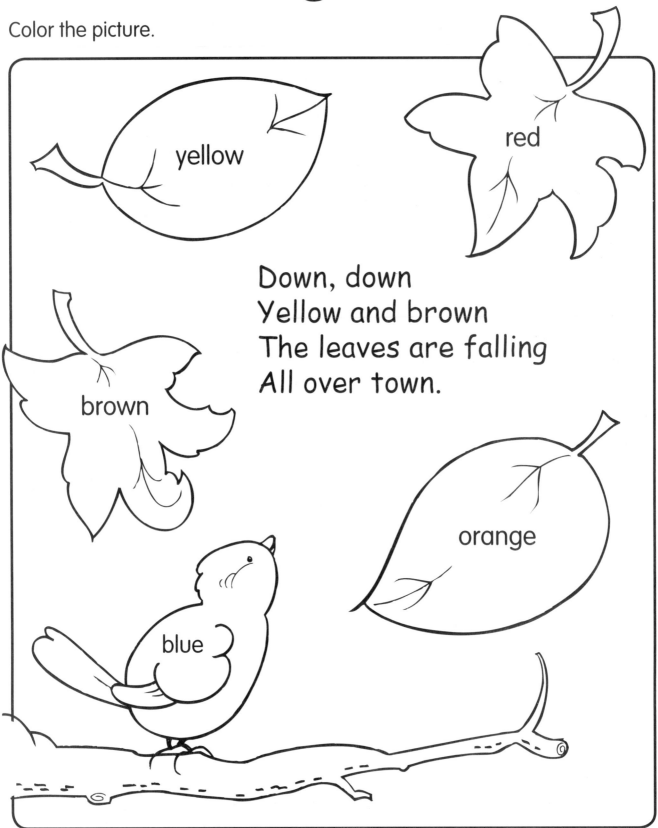

yellow

red

Down, down
Yellow and brown
The leaves are falling
All over town.

brown

orange

blue

 Seasonal Activities • EMC 2002 • © Evan-Moor Corp.

Name _____

Count the Leaves

Trace the numbers.
Color the leaves.

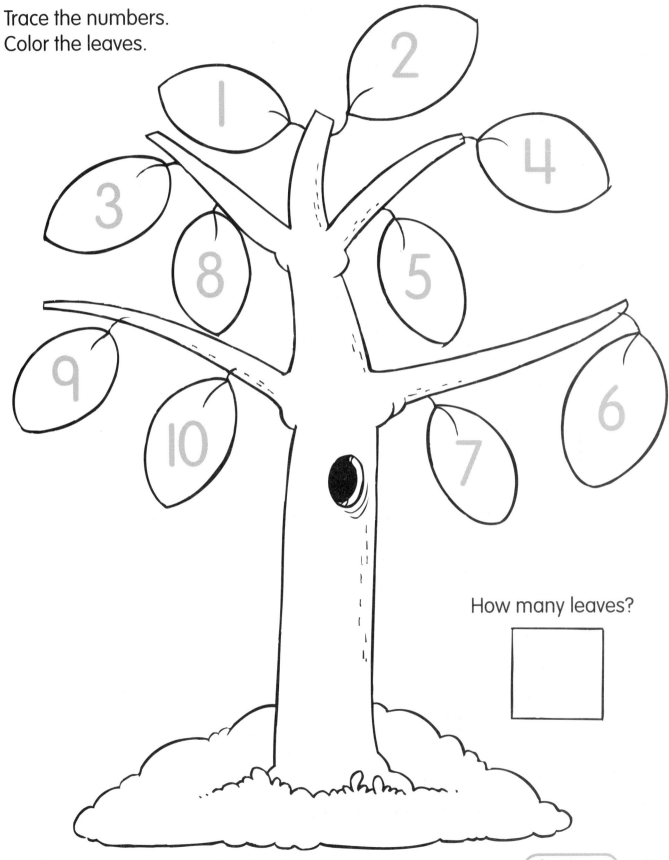

How many leaves?

Name _____

Autumn Bear

Dress the bear
for autumn.

Note: Use these with the bear on page 8.

Color the bear and his clothes.
Cut out the clothes he will wear in the autumn.
Glue them onto the bear.

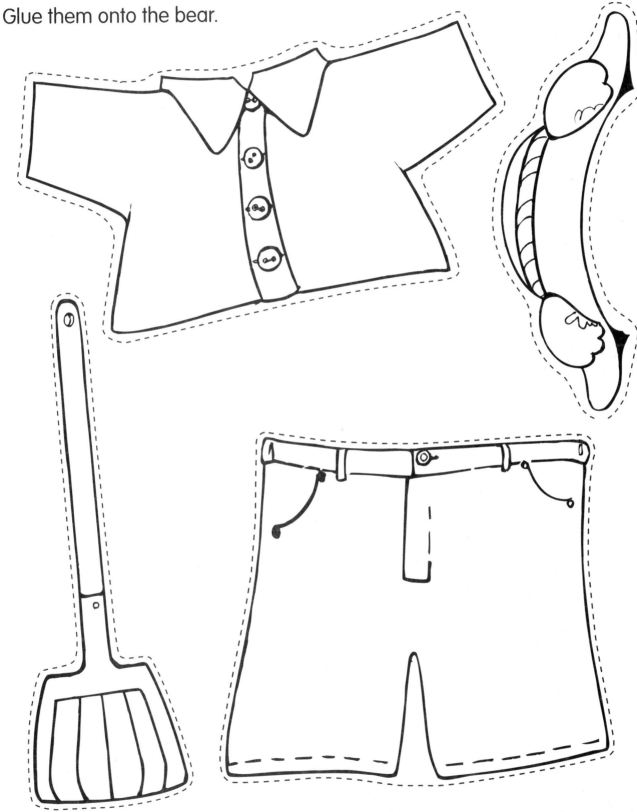

Name _____

It Starts Like "Leaf"

Color the pictures that begin with
the same sound as **leaf**.

leaf

Trace the letters.

     Seasonal Activities • EMC 2002 • © Evan-Moor Corp.

Help the Squirrel

Squirrel is looking for his acorns.
Draw a line to show him the way.

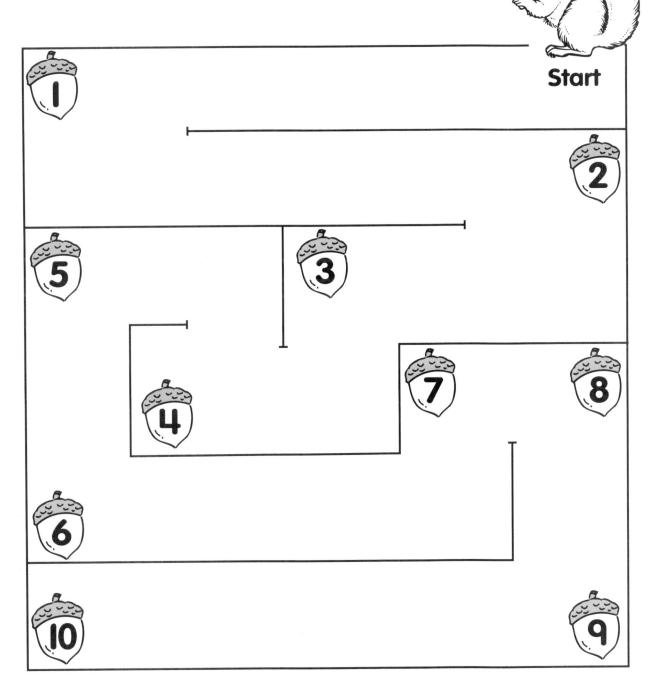

Count Squirrel's acorns. _____

Name _____

Acorns and Leaves

Circle the picture that matches the first one in each row.

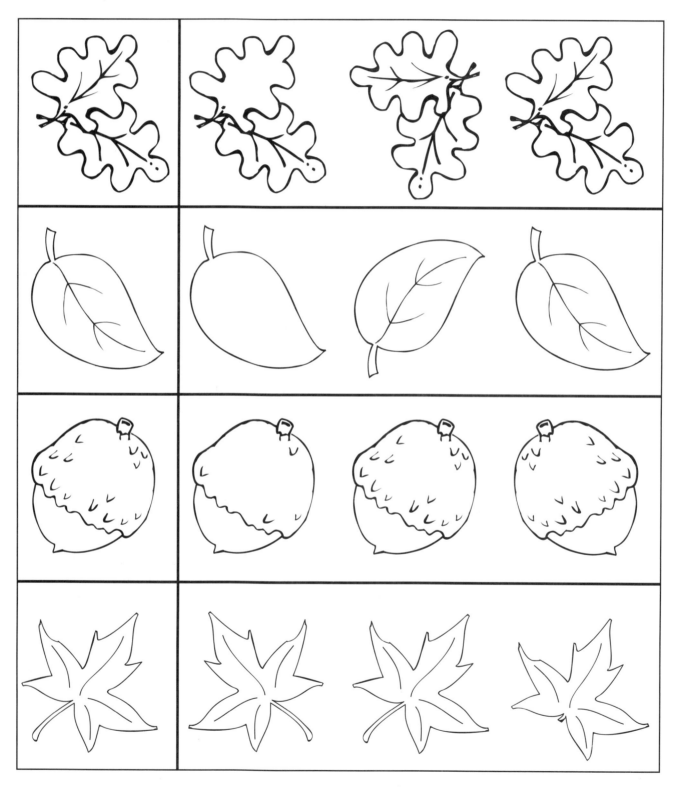

Seasonal Activities • EMC 2002 • © Evan-Moor Corp.

In School

Color the classroom.

Count and write the numbers.

 = ☐   = ☐    = ☐

 = ☐    = ☐   = ☐

Name _____

School Tools

Color the tools you
use at school.

Seasonal Activities • EMC 2002 • © Evan-Moor Corp.

Name _____

Christopher Columbus

Draw a line to help Columbus find his ship.

Start

Columbus sailed the ocean blue.

Trace the letters.   Columbus

The Santa Maria

Color, cut, and glue
to finish the ship.

glue

glue

glue

glue

Columbus sailed to America.
His ship was named the *Santa Maria*.

Seasonal Activities • EMC 2002 • © Evan-Moor Corp.

Note: Reproduce this page to use with page 16.

sails

Christopher Columbus

sailors

Note: Reproduce this page to use with page 16.

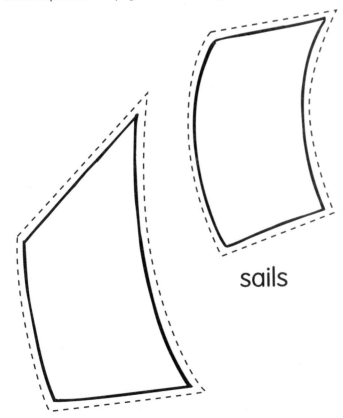

sails

Christopher Columbus

sailors

It Starts Like "Pumpkin"

Glue the pictures that begin with
the same sound as **pumpkin**.

glue	glue
glue	glue
glue	glue

Trace the letters.

pumpkin

Note: Use these pictures with page 18.

Note: Use these pictures with page 18.

The Scarecrow

Cut out the puzzle. Glue the pieces inside the frame.

glue	glue
glue	glue

Trace the letters.

scarecrow

Seasonal Activities • EMC 2002 • © Evan-Moor Corp.

Note: Reproduce this puzzle to use with the frame on page 20.

Watch the Pumpkin Grow

Cut out the pictures. Glue them in order.

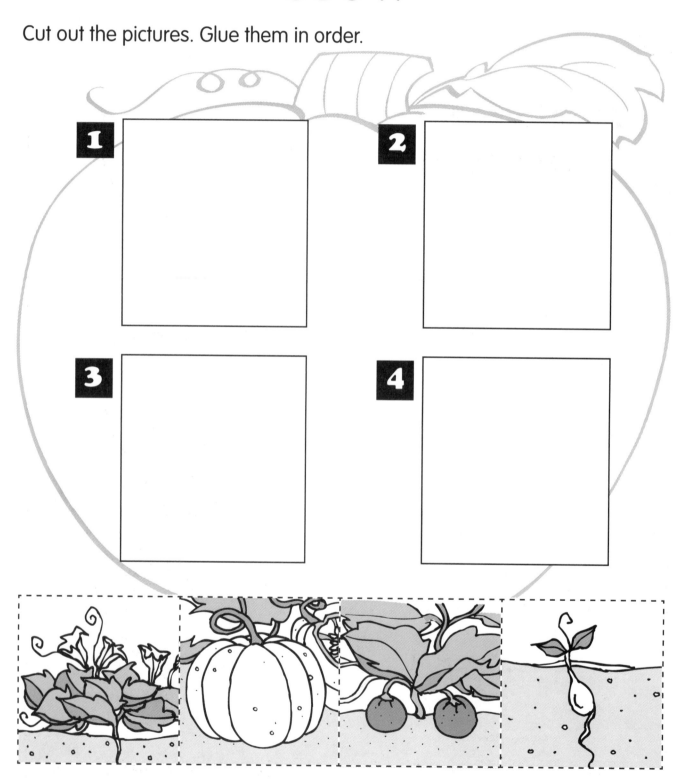

Seasonal Activities • EMC 2002 • © Evan-Moor Corp.

Halloween Surprise

Cut on the lines. Put the pages in order. Staple the book together.

Halloween Surprise

staple

1 pumpkin ②

2 eyes ③

3 teeth ④

Funny jack-o'-lantern! ⑤

Let's trick or treat! ⑥

Name _____

My Pumpkin

Start at 1.
Connect the dots.

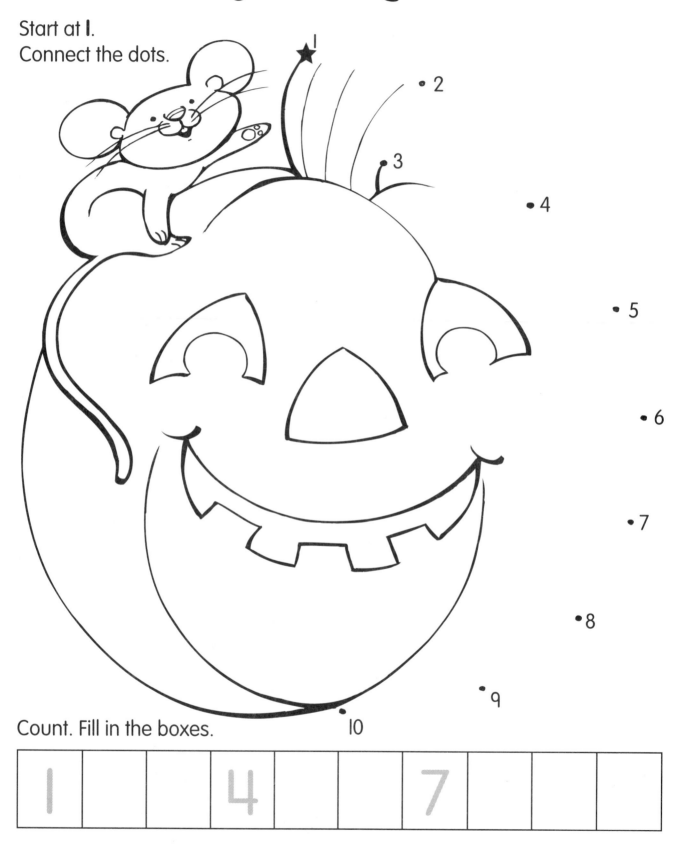

Count. Fill in the boxes.

1			4			7			

Seasonal Activities • EMC 2002 • © Evan-Moor Corp.

Name _____

What Is It?

Color: **1**—green   **2**—orange   **3**—yellow   **4**—blue

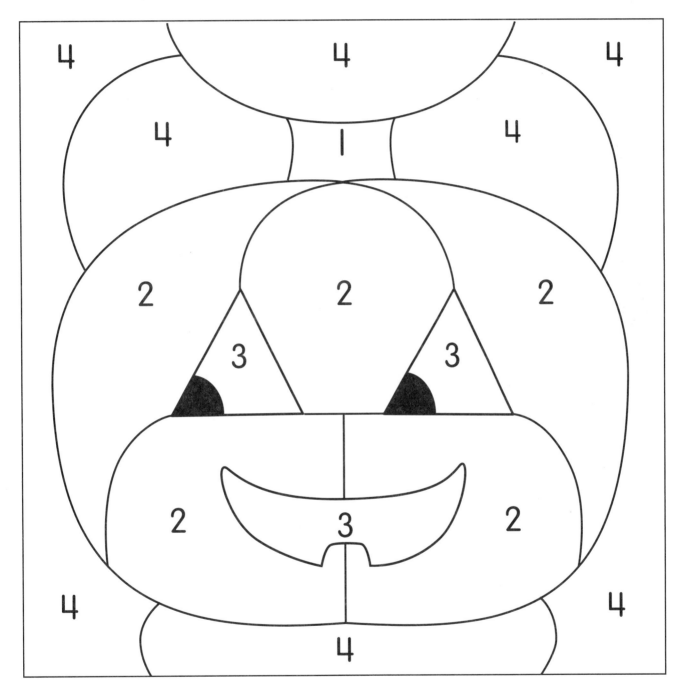

It is a pumpkin.   ☺ yes   ☹ no

It is orange.   ☺ yes   ☹ no

Name _____

10 Little Goblins

Trace the numbers.

	1 little 2 little 3 little goblins
	4 little 5 little 6 little goblins
	7 little 8 little 9 little goblins
	10 little goblins here

Seasonal Activities • EMC 2002 •

Halloween Match

Circle the picture that is the same as the first one in each row.

Trick or Treat?

Match the goblins to their treat bags.

Seasonal Activities • EMC 2002 • © Evan-Moor Corp.

Name _____

Bat

Color, cut, and glue the ones that rhyme with **bat**.

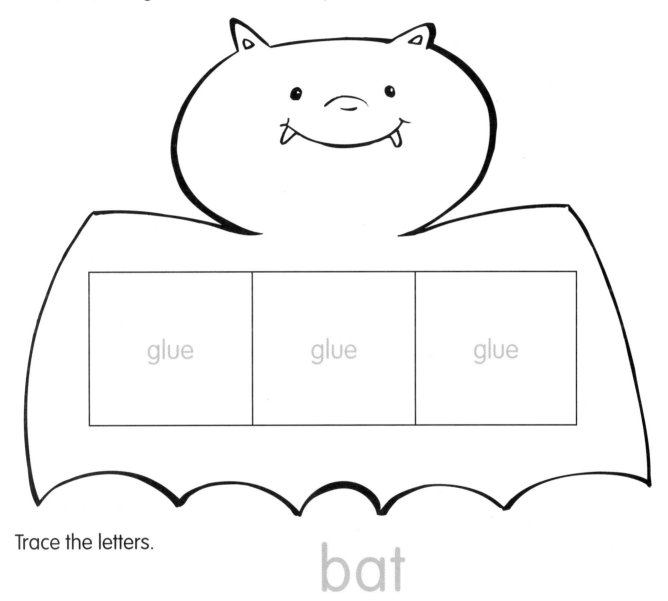

| glue | glue | glue |

Trace the letters.

bat

Thanksgiving

Cut on the lines. Put the pages in order. Staple the book together.

Thanksgiving Word Book

staple

Mayflower

2

Pilgrims

3

Thanksgiving dinner

4

Seasonal Activities • EMC 2002 • © Evan-Moor Corp.

Name _____

The Mayflower

Connect the dots. Color the ship.

The Pilgrims came on the *Mayflower*.

Trace the letters.

Mayflower

Name _____

A Pilgrim Family

Color the Pilgrims. Cut and glue to finish the picture.

glue

glue

glue

Father

Mother

Child

Seasonal Activities • EMC 2002 • © Evan-Moor Corp.

Name _____

Squanto

Color Squanto and the Pilgrim.

Squanto was a Native American.
He helped the Pilgrims.
He showed them how to plant corn.

Trace the letters.

Squanto

Mr. Turkey

Cut out the puzzle. Glue the pieces inside the frame.

glue	glue
glue	glue

Trace.

See the turkey.

Seasonal Activities • EMC 2002 • © Evan-Moor Corp.

Note: Use this puzzle with the frame on page 34.

Name _____

It Starts Like "Turkey"

Color the pictures that begin with the same sound as **turkey**.

Trace the letters.

I see a turkey.

Seasonal Activities • EMC 2002 • © Evan-Moor Corp.

Name _____

Thanksgiving Match

Color the picture that matches the first one in each row.

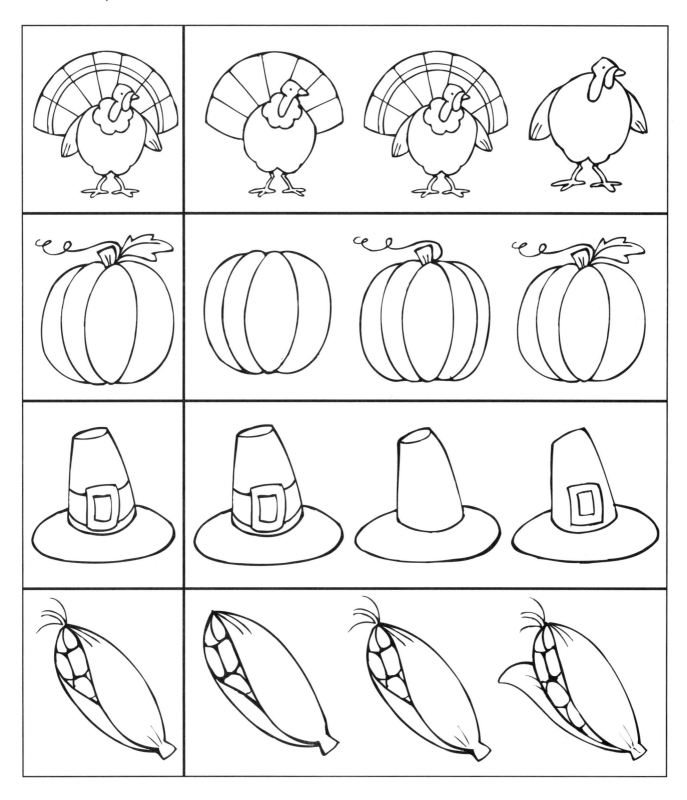

Name _____

Thanksgiving Dinner

Draw what you eat on Thanksgiving Day.

Trace.

Happy Thanksgiving!

 Seasonal Activities • EMC 2002 • © Evan-Moor Corp.

At-Home Activities

Winter Weather

Winter Holidays

Winter

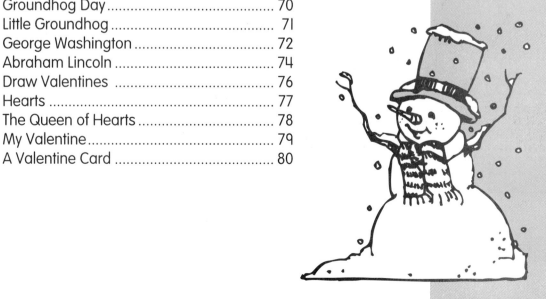

Name _____

December
At-Home Activities

Parents, please post this chart at home.
Check off activities as you complete them.

Week 1

☐ Read a book together. Ask your child to retell the story.

☐ Ask your child to count the windows in your house.

☐ Play "Follow the Leader" with your child. Include hopping, skipping, jumping, etc.

Week 2

☐ Read a book together. Ask your child to tell you about his or her favorite part.

☐ Take ten shoes of different sizes. Ask your child to put them in order from smallest to largest.

☐ Take a walk around the neighborhood. Look for letters, numbers, and words.

Week 3

☐ Read a book together. Ask your child to name the characters in the story.

☐ Help your child name the objects and furniture in his or her bedroom.

☐ Have your child fold and place a napkin by each plate to help set the table for dinner.

Week 4

☐ Read a book together. Ask your child to act out something that happened in the story.

☐ Play "I Am Thinking of an Animal." Give the clues at first, then ask your child to give clues about an animal. "I'm thinking of an animal that has four legs. It has fur. It meows." (answer: a cat)

☐ Play a board game or a card game together as a family.

Seasonal Activities • EMC 2002 • © Evan-Moor Corp.

Name _____

January
At-Home Activities

Parents, please post this chart at home.
Check off activities as you complete them.

Week 1

☐ Read a book together. Ask your child to retell the story.

☐ Help your child find objects around the house and yard that begin with the same sound as *duck*.

☐ Play "beanbag toss" with your child. (You can make a beanbag by tying rice or beans in a sock.) Ask your child to try to toss the beanbag into a wastebasket; to toss it as far as possible; to toss it in the air and catch it.

Week 2

☐ Read a book together. Ask your child to tell you about his or her favorite part.

☐ Have your child help make his or her bed.

☐ Take a "shape walk" around the neighborhood. See how many different things that are round, square, or rectangular your child can find. Identify unusual shapes such as the hexagon of a traffic sign for your child.

Week 3

☐ Read a book together. Ask your child to name the characters in the story.

☐ Encourage your child to draw a picture of his or her favorite animal.

☐ Have your child try to count to 30. Give help when needed.

Week 4

☐ Read a book together. Ask your child to act out something that happened in the story.

☐ Have your child help fix a breakfast of cereal, fruit, and milk. Talk about the ingredients and tools you use.

☐ Play a board game or a card game together as a family.

Name _____

February
At-Home Activities

Parents, please post this chart at home.
Check off activities as you complete them.

Week 1

- [ ] Read a book together. Ask your child to retell the story.
- [ ] Encourage your child to count to 40. Give help when it is needed.
- [ ] Cut the bottoms off two large plastic containers. Use them to play catch with a softball or beanbag.

Week 2

- [ ] Read a book together. Ask your child to tell you about his or her favorite part.
- [ ] Help your child name different plants in your yard or a nearby park.
- [ ] Take an "animal walk" around the neighborhood. Check in trees for birds and squirrels. Check the ground for worms and insects. Look around for pet animals.

Week 3

- [ ] Read a book together. Ask your child to name the characters in the story.
- [ ] Help your child find objects around the house and yard that begin with the same sound as *sock*.
- [ ] Ask your child to name all of the people in your family by relationship (brother) and by name (Max).

Week 4

- [ ] Read a book together. Ask your child to act out something that happened in the story.
- [ ] Make fruit kabobs with your child (including one or two new fruits). Ask your child to name the fruits and describe how they look and taste.
- [ ] Play a board game or a card game together as a family.

Seasonal Activities • EMC 2002 • © Evan-Moor Corp.

Winter Word Book

Cut on the lines. Put the pages in order. Staple the book together.

staple

Winter Is Here!

mittens 2

jacket 3

boots 4

snow 5

fun 6

Name _____

Winter Bear

Color the bear and
his clothes.

Note: Use these with the bear on page 44.

Cut out the clothes he needs for the winter.

Dress the bear for winter.

Name _____

It's Snowing!

Cut out the puzzle. Glue the pieces inside the frame.

glue

glue

glue

glue

Trace the letters.

See the snow.

Seasonal Activities • EMC 2002 • © Evan-Moor Corp.

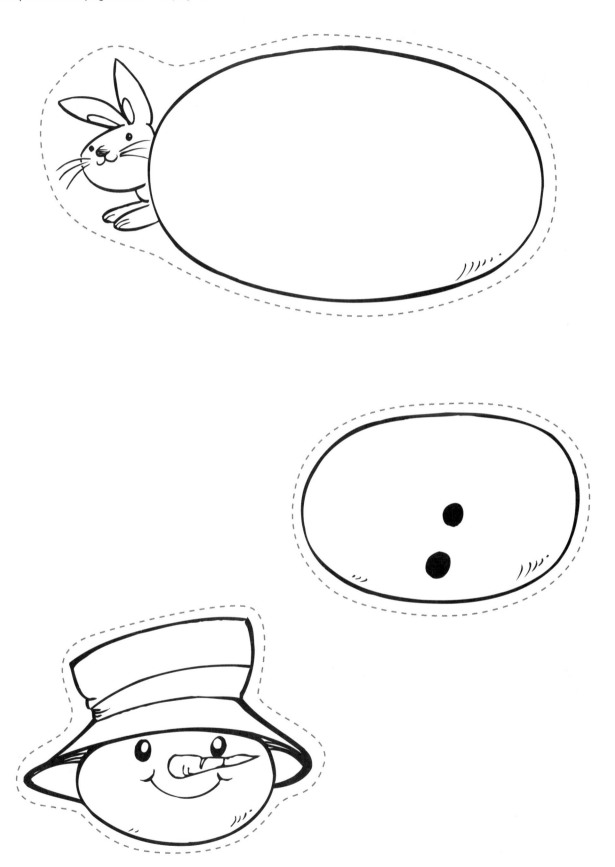

Name _____

Down a Snowy Hill

Draw a line to help the girl down the hill.

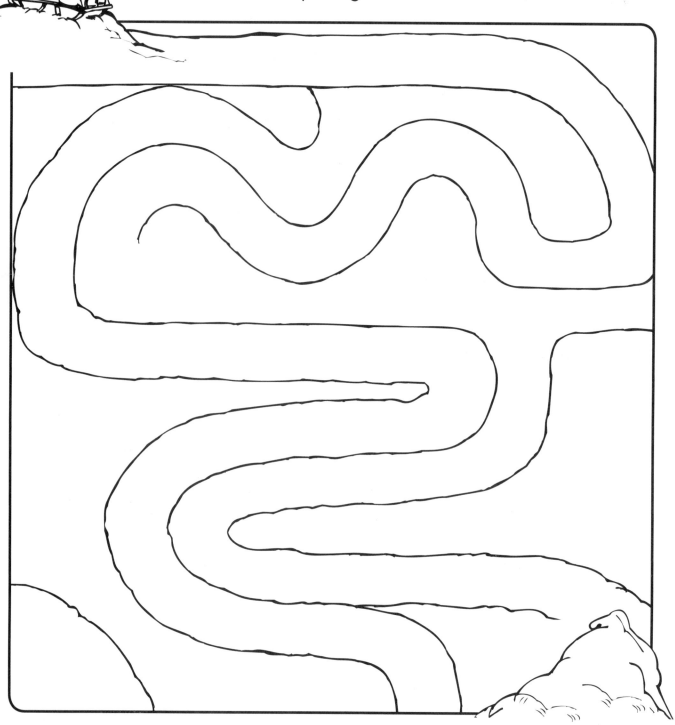

Trace the letters.

The sled is red.

Seasonal Activities • EMC 2002 • © Evan-Moor Corp.

What Is Missing?

This is a snowman.

Draw the missing parts.

Trace the letters.

See the snowman.

Holiday Candles

Cut on the lines. Put the pages in order. Staple the book together.

staple

Candles

Christmas candles

2

Hanukkah candles

3

Kwanzaa candles

4

Name _____

The First Christmas

Cut out the missing pieces. Glue them in the picture.

glue

glue

glue

Mary had a baby.

Name _____

O, Christmas Tree

Color the Christmas tree. Count the types of ornaments.

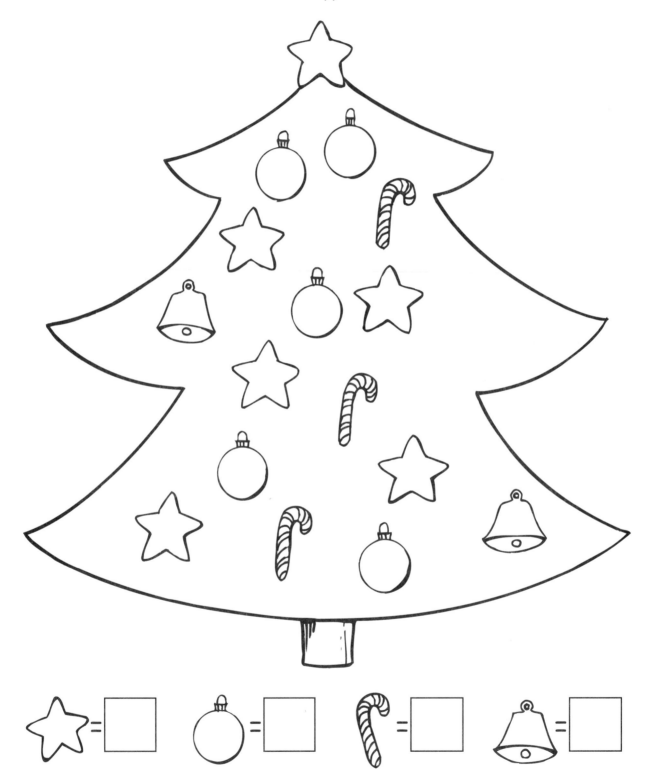

Seasonal Activities • EMC 2002 • © Evan-Moor Corp.

Surprise!

Match the gift to the package.

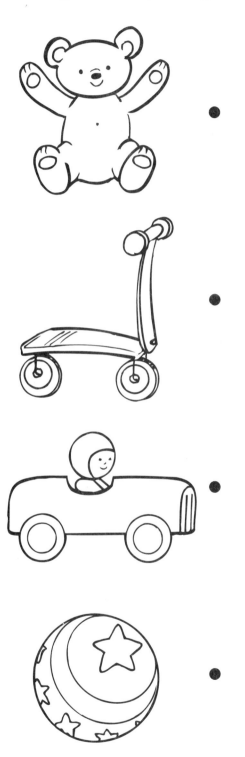

Name _____

Here Comes Santa

Draw a line to help Santa find the house.

Trace the letters.

I see Santa.

Seasonal Activities • EMC 2002 • © Evan-Moor Corp.

Name _____

Christmas Stocking

Start at **I**. Connect the dots. Color the picture.

Santa's Bag

Color Santa Claus. Draw a surprise in Santa's bag.

Trace.

See the surprise.

Seasonal Activities • EMC 2002 • © Evan-Moor Corp.

Name _____

Santa's Reindeer

Count and color the reindeer.

Trace. I see ___ reindeer.

A Menorah for Hanukkah

Trace the numbers. Color the candles.

Light one candle every night.
The menorah spreads a special light.

Write the missing numbers.

1 _____ _____ _____ 5 _____ _____ _____ _____

   Seasonal Activities • EMC 2002 • © Evan-Moor Corp.

Name _____

Spin, Dreidel, Spin

See the dreidel spin.

Count the dreidels. Write the number.

Name _____

Kwanzaa

Count the candles on the kinara.
Color the candles.

1 red
2 red
3 red
4 black
5 green
6 green
7 green

See the kinara.
It is Kwanzaa.

Trace the letters.   See the kinara.

   Seasonal Activities • EMC 2002 • © Evan-Moor Corp.

Name _____

A Kwanzaa Placemat

Cut out the corn.
Glue it to the placemat.

One ear of corn for each child in the family.

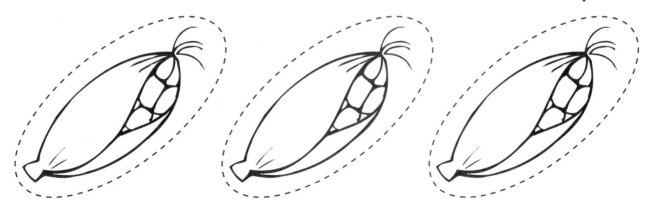

Name _____

Happy New Year!

Connect the dots.
Trace and write the numbers for the year.

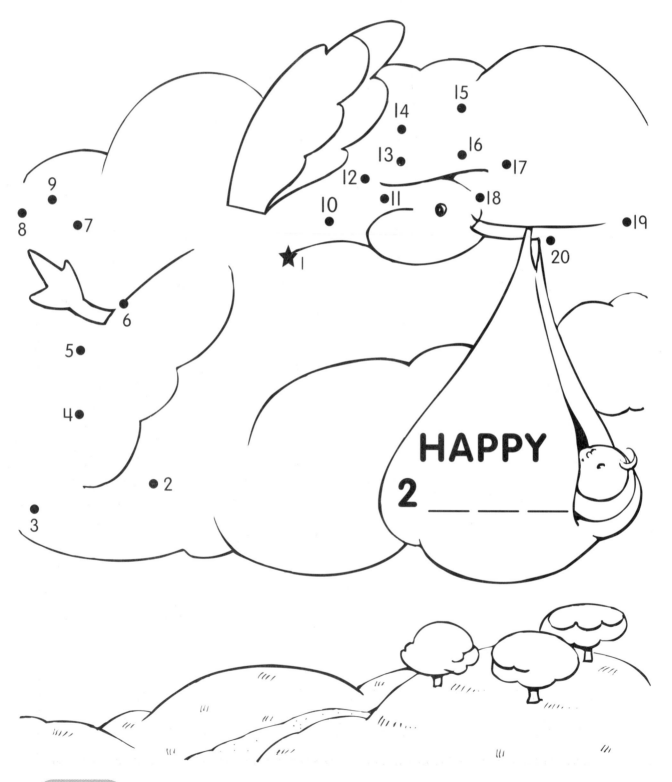

Seasonal Activities • EMC 2002 • © Evan-Moor Corp.

Name _____

He Had a Dream

Color the picture.

Martin Luther King, Jr., had a dream.
He wanted everyone to be treated fairly.

Name _____

Martin Luther King, Jr.

Cut out the puzzle. Glue the pieces inside the frame.

glue	glue
glue	glue

He was a good man.
He was a brave man.
He was a fair man.

Seasonal Activities • EMC 2002 • © Evan-Moor Corp.

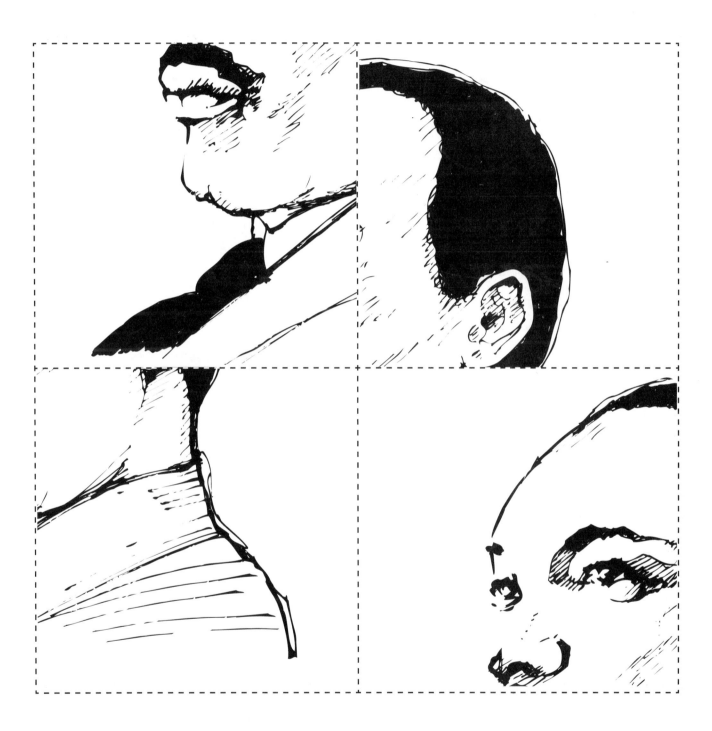

Groundhog Day

Cut on the dotted lines. Fold on solid lines so page 1 is in front.

Seasonal Activities • EMC 2002 • © Evan-Moor Corp.

Little Groundhog

Color the picture. Fold on the lines. See the groundhog pop up.

1 fold up

Happy Groundhog Day

2 fold up

Name _____

George Washington

Cut out the puzzle. Glue the pieces inside the frame.

glue	glue	glue
glue	glue	glue

Washington was the first president of the United States. George Washington's face is on the quarter.

Seasonal Activities • EMC 2002 • © Evan-Moor Corp.

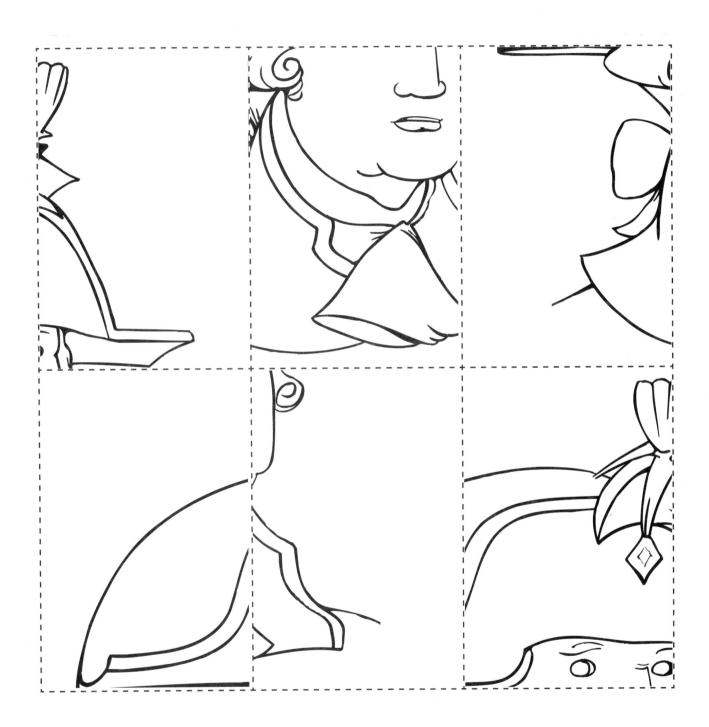

Abraham Lincoln

Cut out the puzzle. Glue the pieces inside the frame.

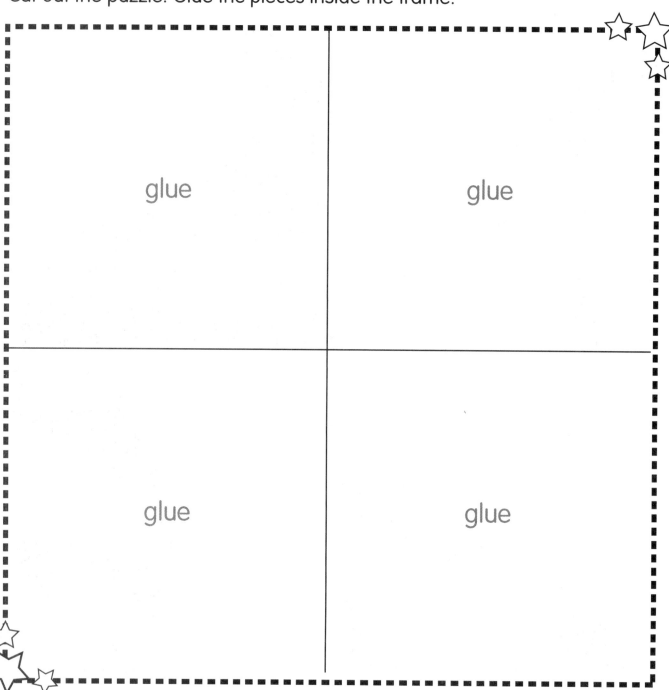

glue   glue

glue   glue

Lincoln was the 16th president of the
United States. Abraham Lincoln's face
is on the penny.

    Seasonal Activities • EMC 2002 • © Evan-Moor Corp.

Name _____

Draw Valentines

Make the second valentine like the first one.

Name _____

Hearts

Find the hearts. Color them.

Circle how many you found.

1 2 3 4 5 6 7 8 9 10

The Queen of Hearts

Color the tart red. Draw three more tarts.

The queen of hearts
Baked some tarts.

 Seasonal Activities • EMC 2002 • © Evan-Moor Corp.

Name _____

My Valentine

Color the heart. Cut and paste the words in order.

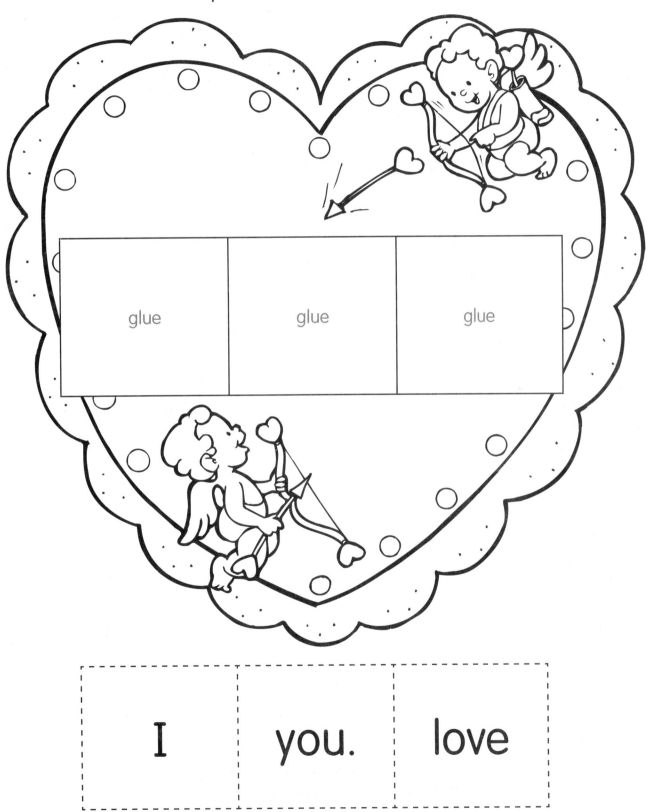

| glue | glue | glue |

| I | you. | love |

Name _____

A Valentine Card

Color the valentine card.
Trace the words. Cut it out.
Give it to a friend.

Be My
Valentine

Name:

Seasonal Activities • EMC 2002 • © Evan-Moor Corp.

Name _____

March
At-Home Activities

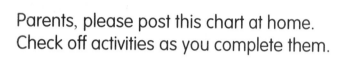

Parents, please post this chart at home.
Check off activities as you complete them.

Week 1

- [ ] Read a book together. Ask your child to retell the story.

- [ ] Ask your child to sort coins by types (penny, nickel, dime) and then name each type of coin.

- [ ] Play "Do What I Do." Act out a motion (hop, jump, fly, swim, etc.). Ask your child to copy the motion.

Week 2

- [ ] Read a book together. Ask your child to tell you about his or her favorite part.

- [ ] Take several pieces of fruit and make a simple pattern (apple, orange, apple, orange). Ask your child to copy the pattern. Repeat with a more difficult pattern (apple, apple, orange, apple, apple, orange).

- [ ] Take a walk through the house and have your child name each room and explain how it is used by the family.

Week 3

- [ ] Read a book together. Ask your child to name the characters in the story.

- [ ] Ask your child to draw a picture of your house and yard.

- [ ] Have your child help make his or her sandwich for lunch. Talk about the ingredients and tools you use.

Week 4

- [ ] Read a book together. Ask your child to act out something that happened in the story.

- [ ] Take your child shopping at the market. Give him or her a job to do such as choose the fruit for the family or count out a certain number of items into a bag.

- [ ] Play a board game or a card game together as a family.

Seasonal Activities • EMC 2002 • © Evan-Moor Corp.

Name _____

April
At-Home Activities

Parents, please post this chart at home.
Check off activities as you complete them.

Week 1

☐ Read a book together. Ask your child to retell the story.

☐ Play the "rhyming game." Say two words. Have your child decide if the words rhyme; "up, cup" "Yes, they rhyme"; "up, in" "No, they don't rhyme."

☐ Put on some music and dance with your child.

Week 2

☐ Read a book together. Ask your child to tell you about his or her favorite part.

☐ Help your child write a note to a favorite friend or family member. Mail the note together (at the post office, if possible).

☐ Take a walk around the neighborhood. Look for letters, numbers, and words.

Week 3

☐ Read a book together. Ask your child to name the characters in the story.

☐ Help your child name the various types of clothing in his or her closet.

☐ Have your child recite the alphabet for you. Provide help as needed.

Week 4

☐ Read a book together. Ask your child to act out something that happened in the story.

☐ Play "I Am Thinking of a Vegetable (or fruit)." Give the clues at first, then ask your child to give clues. "I'm thinking of a fruit that is long and yellow. Its skin peels off easily." (answer: a banana)

☐ Play a board game or a card game together as a family.

Name _____

May
At-Home Activities

Parents, please post this chart at home.
Check off activities as you complete them.

Week 1

- [ ] Read a book together. Ask your child to retell the story.

- [ ] Help your child find objects around the house and yard that begin with the same sound as *toy*.

- [ ] Hop, skip, and jump around the yard with your child.

Week 2

- [ ] Read a book together. Ask your child to tell you about his or her favorite part.

- [ ] Select two of your child's favorite toys. Ask your child to explain how the two toys are different. Then ask him or her to tell how the toys are alike.

- [ ] Take a walk together in an area with shops and other businesses. Look at each building as you pass by. Talk about what kind of business it is used for. (This is a grocery store. Food is sold here. That is a gas station. You can fill your gas tank there.)

Week 3

- [ ] Read a book together. Ask your child to name the characters in the story.

- [ ] Give your child a pile of buttons of different kinds to sort into sets. The sets may be by color, size, or the number of holes in the button.

- [ ] Make instant pudding together. Talk about the ingredients and tools you use.

Week 4

- [ ] Read a book together. Ask your child to act out something that happened in the story.

- [ ] Ask your child to explain step by step how to brush teeth, beginning with "take the toothpaste."

- [ ] Play a board game or a card game together as a family.

Seasonal Activities • EMC 2002 • © Evan-Moor Corp.

Name _____

It's Spring

Color. Fold.

It's
Spring!

Birds are peeping
Chicks are cheeping
Gardens sprouting
Children shouting

Jill Norris

-1-fold up-

-2-fold down-

Spring Weather

Cut on the lines. Fold twice so that page 1 is in front.

2 — April showers

1 — Spring Weather — March winds

fold 1

fold 2

3 — May flowers

4 — It's Spring!

Seasonal Activities • EMC 2002 • © Evan-Moor Corp.

March Winds

Cut out the missing pieces. Glue them in the picture.

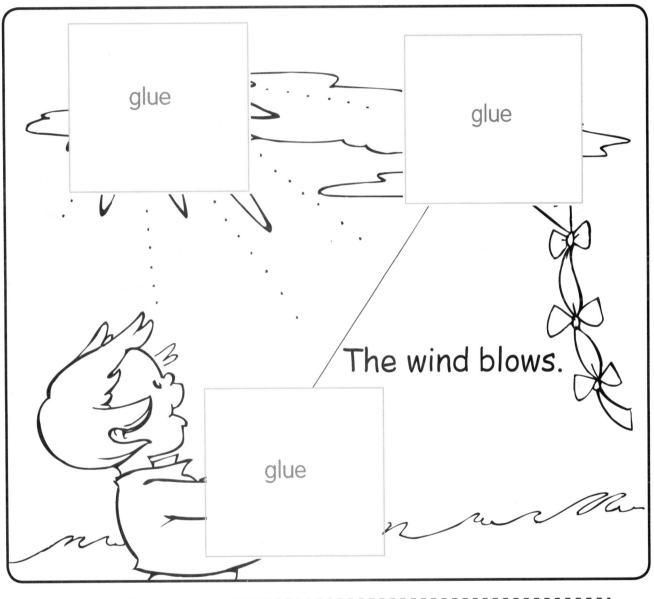

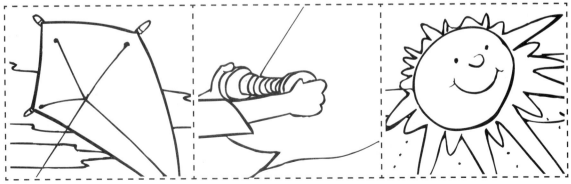

Name _____

Up, Up, and Away

Start at **I**. Connect the dots. Color the picture.

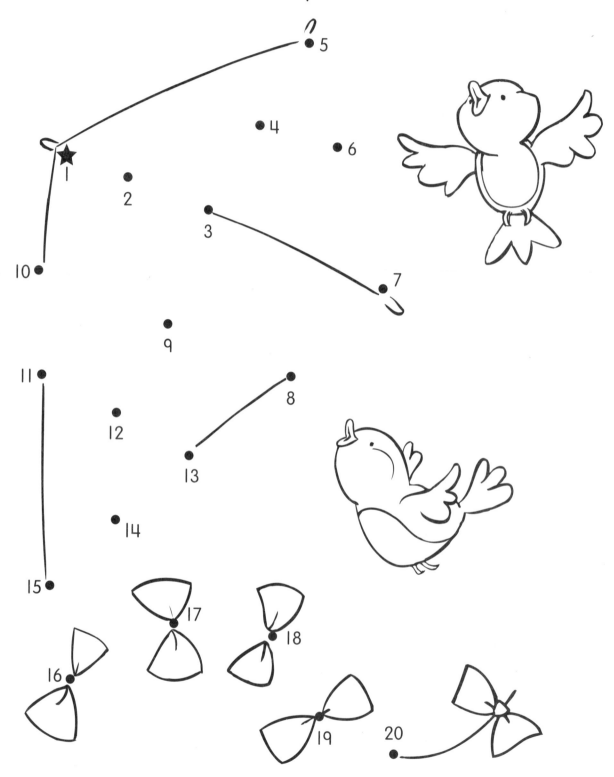

Seasonal Activities • EMC 2002 • © Evan-Moor Corp.

Name _____

Kites

Make the kites the same in each row.

Name _____

Rain, Rain

Glue the top of the bear's umbrella here.

glue top here

It is raining cats and dogs!

Trace the letters. See the rain.

Seasonal Activities • EMC 2002 • © Evan-Moor Corp.

Note: Reproduce the umbrella to use with page 90.

Glue the **top** of the umbrella over the art on page 90, then lift it up to see the message underneath.

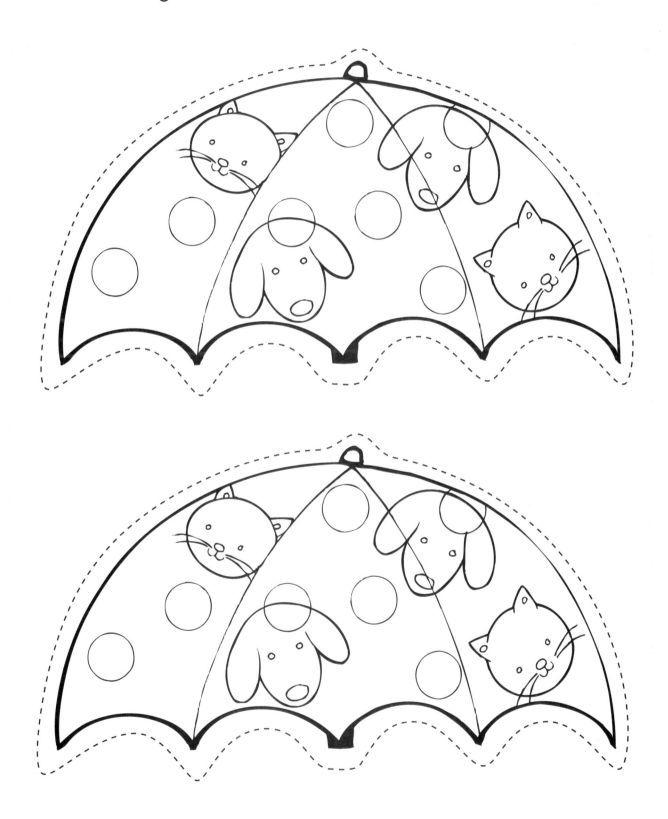

April Showers

Cut out the puzzle. Glue the pieces inside the frame.

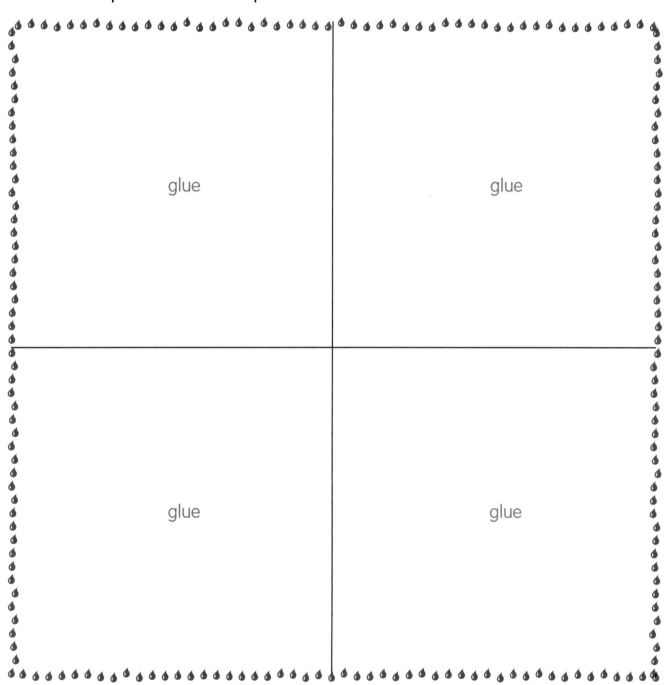

Rain is water that falls from the clouds.
Rain falls in drops.

     Seasonal Activities • EMC 2002 • © Evan-Moor Corp.

Note: Reproduce this puzzle to use with page 92.

Name _____

It Rhymes with "Rain"

Color the pictures that rhyme with **rain**.

rain

Seasonal Activities • EMC 2002 • © Evan-Moor Corp.

Name _____

Seed to Flower

Cut out the pictures. Glue them in order.

glue	glue	glue

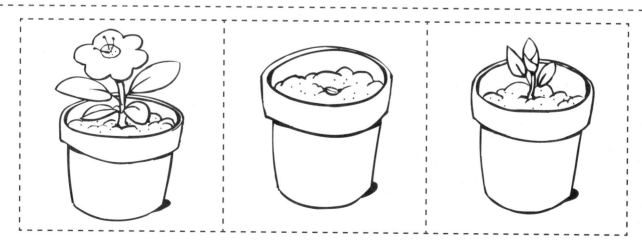

May Flowers

Count the petals and write the number in the center. Color the flowers.

Fill in the missing numbers.

1		3		5			8		10

Seasonal Activities • EMC 2002 • © Evan-Moor Corp.

Name _____

Mothers and Babies

Many babies are born in the spring. Draw a line to make a match.

Trace the letters.

The baby is little.

Name _____

In the Spring

Mother bird lays her eggs in the nest.

Glue the babies in the nest. Count the birds.

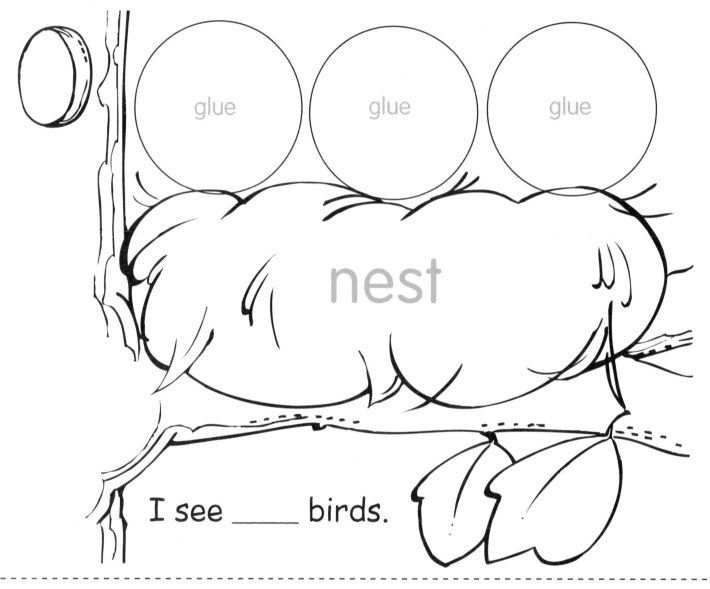

glue   glue   glue

nest

I see ___ birds.

  Seasonal Activities • EMC 2002 • © Evan-Moor Corp.

A Butterfly Grows

Cut out the pictures. Glue them in order.

Fly away, butterfly!

1

2

3

| glue | glue | glue |

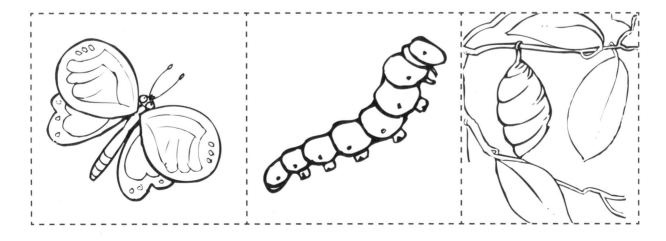

Name _____

Butterfly Fun

Draw to match.

Seasonal Activities • EMC 2002 • © Evan-Moor Corp.

Johnny Appleseed

Johnny Appleseed lived long ago.
He planted apple trees wherever he would go.

Find the apples. Color them.

I found _____ 🍎s.

Name _____

A Big Red Apple

Start at 1.
Connect the dots.
Color the picture.

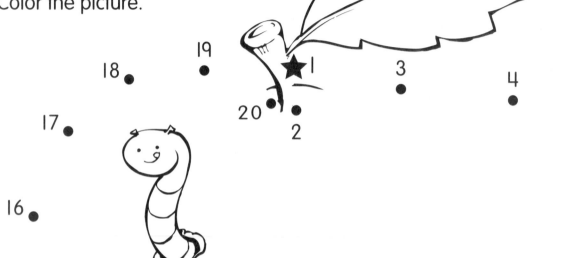

19

18

3

4

20

2

17

5

16

15

6

14

7

13

8

12

11

10

9

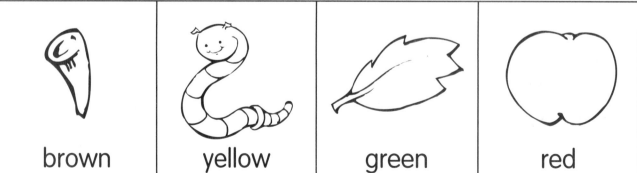

| brown | yellow | green | red |

Seasonal Activities • EMC 2002 • © Evan-Moor Corp.

Name _____

Pot of Gold

Draw a line to help the leprechaun find the pot of gold.

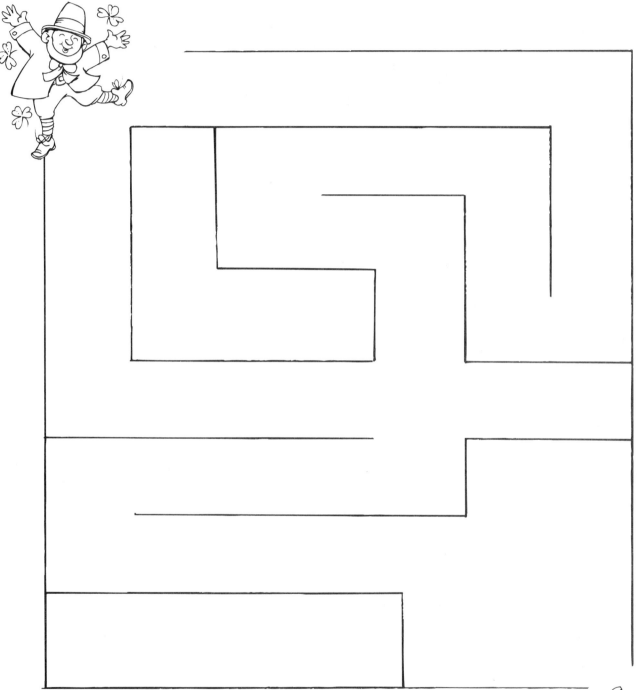

Trace the letters.

pot   gold

Name —————————————

Lucky Shamrocks

Find the shamrocks. Color them green.

shamrock

How many shamrocks did you find?

1 2 3 4 5 6 7 8 9 10

Seasonal Activities • EMC 2002 • © Evan-Moor Corp.

Name _____

Easter Morning

Draw a line to take the family to church.

Trace the letters.

Happy Easter

Fill the Baskets

Draw the Easter eggs.

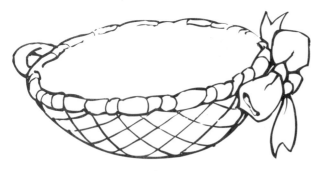

I red egg

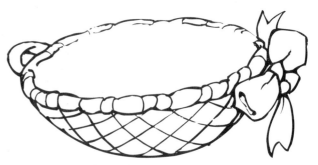

2 blue eggs

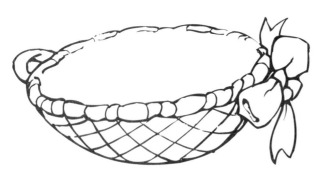

3 yellow eggs

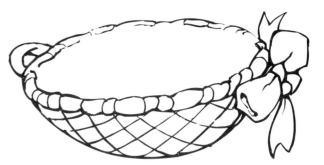

4 purple eggs

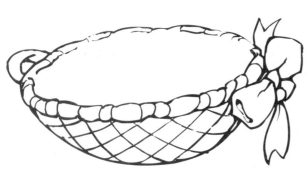

5 green eggs

Seasonal Activities • EMC 2002 • © Evan-Moor Corp.

Name _____

Easter Eggs

Cut out the pictures.
Glue them in order.

1 glue

2 glue

3 glue

Spring 107

Easter Rabbit

Cut out the puzzle.
Glue the pieces inside the frame.

glue

glue

glue

See the Easter rabbit.
He has a big Easter egg.

Note: Reproduce this puzzle to use with the frame on page 108.

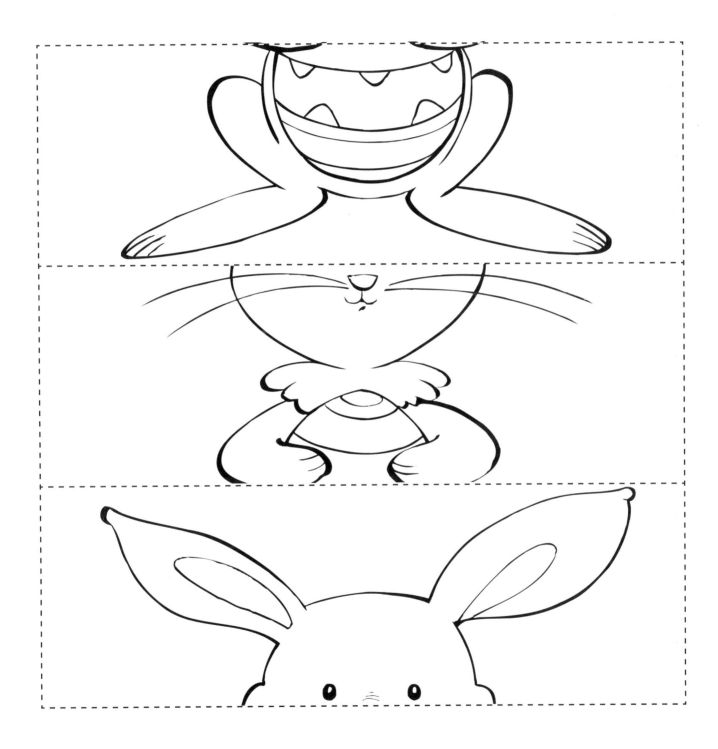

Name _____

How Many Eggs?

Count the eggs.
Color them.

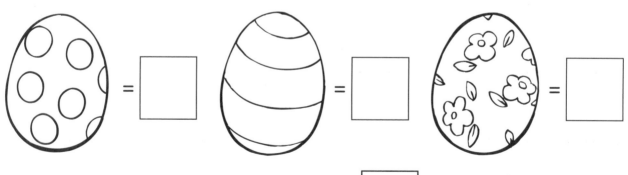

How many in all?

Seasonal Activities • EMC 2002 • © Evan-Moor Corp.

Name _____

It Starts Like "Basket"

Color the pictures that begin with
the same sound as **basket**.

Trace the letters.

Name _____

Easter Fun

Circle the picture that is the same as the first one in each row.

Seasonal Activities • EMC 2002 • © Evan-Moor Corp.

Cinco de Mayo

Color the piñata. ☆ = yellow   ♡ = red   ◇ = blue

It is Cinco de Mayo.
We have a piñata.

Fiesta!

Draw a line to help the children get to the fiesta.

**A fiesta is a party.
It is lots of fun.**

Seasonal Activities • EMC 2002 • © Evan-Moor Corp.

May Day

Cut on the lines. Put the pages in order. Staple the book together.

Fill a basket with flowers.

2

Put the basket by the door.
Ring the bell and hide.

3

Happy May Day!

4

Name _____

May Day Surprise

Cut out the puzzle. Glue the pieces inside the frame.

glue	glue
glue	glue

Trace.

Happy May Day!

Note: Reproduce this puzzle to use with page 116.

May Day Basket

Color. Cut it out. Punch a hole.
Add a string.
Hang it up.

Seasonal Activities • EMC 2002 • © Evan-Moor Corp.

Name _____

My Mother

Draw your mother.

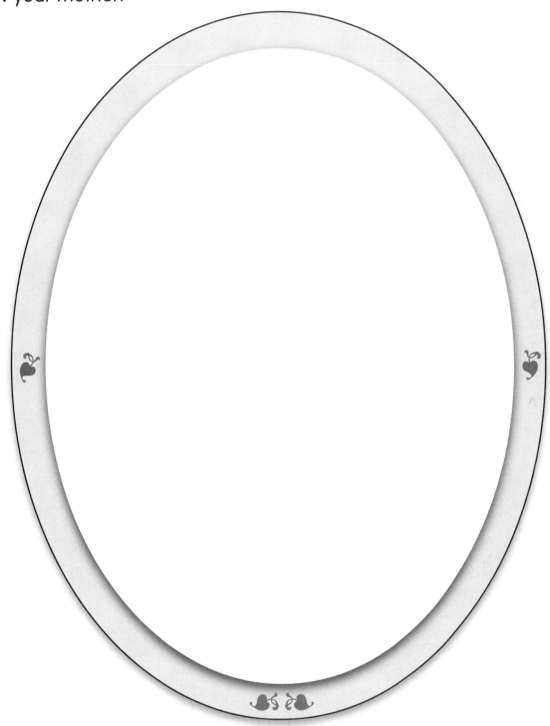

Trace.

Mother

Name _____

Happy Mother's Day

Color the picture. Fold on the lines. See the message pop up.

fold up

I love you.

fold down

Summer

Name _____

June
At-Home Activities

Parents, please post this chart at home.
Check off activities as you complete them.

Week 1

- [ ] Read a book together. Ask your child to retell the story.

- [ ] Help your child find objects around the house and yard that begin with the same sound as *ran*.

- [ ] Play "Do What I Do" with your child. Act out an action (washing dishes, brushing teeth, etc.). Ask your child to identify the action. Then have your child act out an action for you to name.

Week 2

- [ ] Read a book together. Ask your child to tell you about his or her favorite part.

- [ ] Play catch with a ball or beanbag. Try increasing the distance between you and your child as you throw the ball.

- [ ] Ask your child to count aloud to see how high he or she can go. Encourage your child to continue to 50. Give help when needed.

Week 3

- [ ] Read a book together. Ask your child to name the characters in the story.

- [ ] Take a "people" walk around the neighborhood. Ask your child to explain what the different people you see are doing.

- [ ] Encourage your child to draw a picture of his or her best friend. Then have your child explain why he or she likes that friend.

Week 4

- [ ] Read a book together. Ask your child to act out something that happened in the story.

- [ ] Play the "rhyming game." Say two words. Your child decides if the words rhyme: "ring, sing" "Yes, ring and sing rhyme"; "ring, rang" "No, ring and rang don't rhyme."

- [ ] Play a board game or a card game together as a family.

Name _____

July
At-Home Activities

Parents, please post this chart at home.
Check off activities as you complete them.

Week 1

☐ Read a book together. Ask your child to retell the story.

☐ Ask your child to put pennies in sets of ten. Explain that ten pennies are the same amount as one dime.

☐ Play "Animal Follow the Leader" with your child. Act out the movements of different animals (elephant's swaying trunk, bird's flying, kangaroo's hopping, etc.). Your child follows, doing the same movements. Change places and let your child be the leader.

Week 2

☐ Read a book together. Ask your child to tell you about his or her favorite part.

☐ Take six or more plates or bowls of different sizes and ask your child to put them in order from the largest to the smallest.

☐ Make cookies together. Discuss the ingredients and tools you use.

Week 3

☐ Read a book together. Ask your child to name the characters in the story.

☐ Give your child a pile of buttons of different kinds to sort into sets. The sets may be by color, size, or the number of holes in the button.

☐ Make popcorn together. Talk about the ingredients and tools you use.

Week 4

☐ Read a book together. Ask your child to act out something that happened in the story.

☐ Examine items such as milk, eggs, and lettuce in the refrigerator. Discuss where each item comes from. "Where does milk come from? That's right. It comes from a cow."

☐ Play a board game or a card game together as a family.

Name _____

August
At-Home Activities

Parents, please post this chart at home.
Check off activities as you complete them.

Week 1

☐ Read a book together. Ask your child to retell the story.

☐ Ask your child to practice categories by naming 10 of something (fruit, animals, things to wear, etc.).

☐ Help your child practice kicking a ball. Move farther apart as you play together.

Week 2

☐ Read a book together. Ask your child to tell you about his or her favorite part.

☐ Play "I Spy" outdoors using plants, animals, and objects. "I spy something green. It covers the ground. It is soft to walk on."(answer: grass)

☐ Take a walk around the neighborhood. Look for letters, numbers, and words to identify.

Week 3

☐ Read a book together. Ask your child to name the characters in the story.

☐ Have your child draw a self-portrait. Then point to different body parts and clothing for your child to name.

☐ Make Jell-O® together. Talk about the ingredients and tools you use.

☐ Read a book together. Ask your

Week 4

child to act out something that happened in the story.

☐ Using crayons, draw a simple pattern of circles, squares, and triangles. Have your child copy the pattern (circle, square, circle, square, etc.). Then start a pattern and have your child complete it (circle, circle, triangle, circle, circle, triangle, ...).

☐ Play a board game or a card game together as a family.

Name _____

Summer Is Here!

Color the picture.

It is a sunny day.

Name _____

What Will Bear Wear?

Color the bear
and his clothes.

Seasonal Activities • EMC 2002 • © Evan-Moor Corp.

Note: Reproduce the clothes to use with page 126.

Cut out the clothes the bear will wear this summer.
Glue them onto the bear.

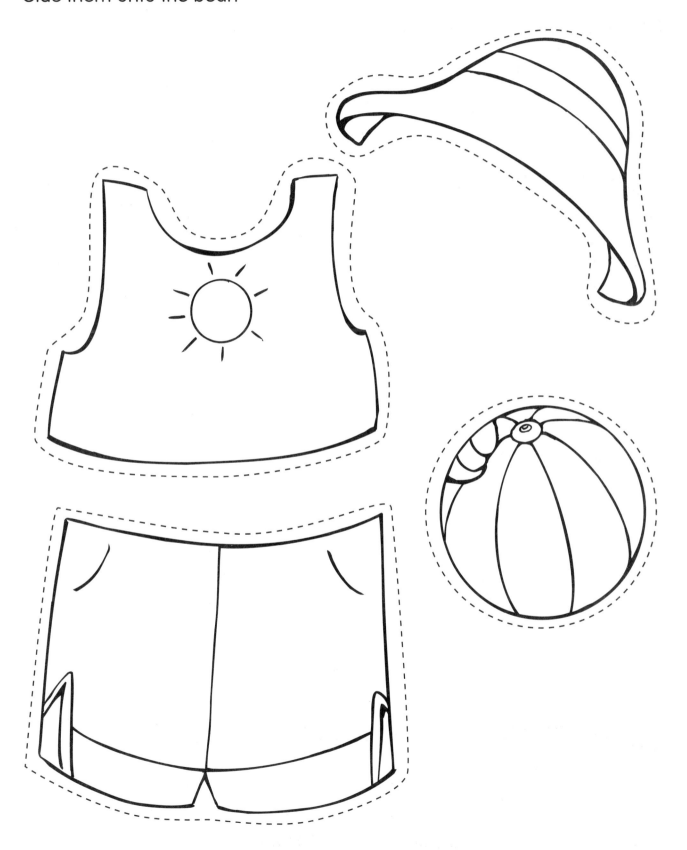

Summer Sun

Start at 1. Connect the dots. Color the sun.

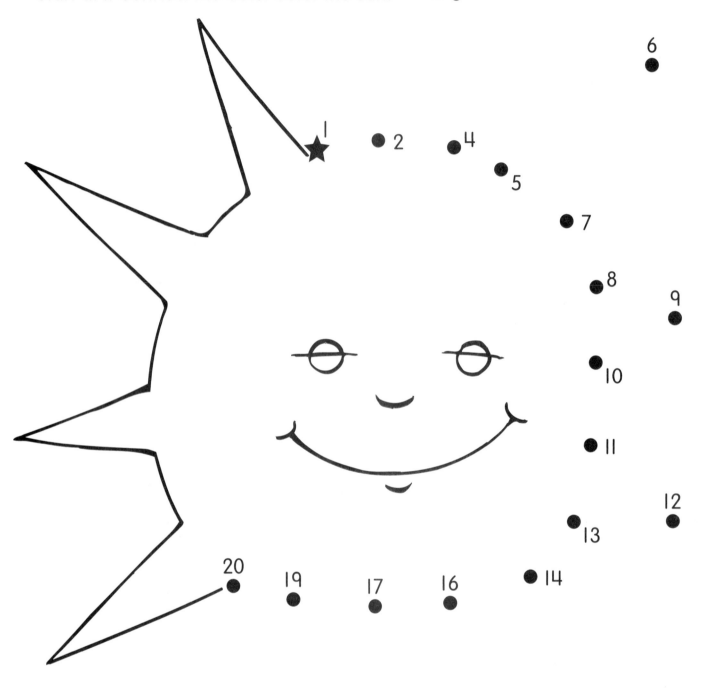

It is so much fun
playing in the summer sun.

Seasonal Activities • EMC 2002 • © Evan-Moor Corp.

Summer Fun

Cut on the lines. Put the pages in order. Staple the book together.

Name _____

Camping

Start at 1. Connect the dots.

It is fun to sleep in a tent.

Seasonal Activities • EMC 2002 • © Evan-Moor Corp.

10 Little Campers

Trace the numbers.

	1 little 2 little 3 little campers
	4 little 5 little 6 little campers
	7 little 8 little 9 little campers
	10 little campers here

By the Sea

What fun
   it will be
To play
   by the sea.

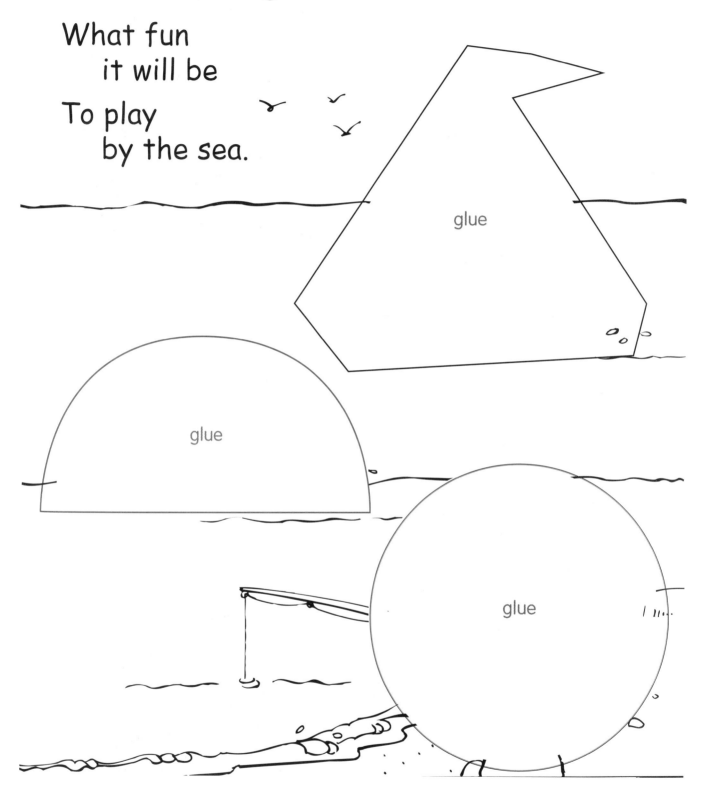

glue

glue

glue

Seasonal Activities • EMC 2002 • © Evan-Moor Corp.

Note: Reproduce these pictures to use on page 132.

Color. Cut. Glue onto page 132.

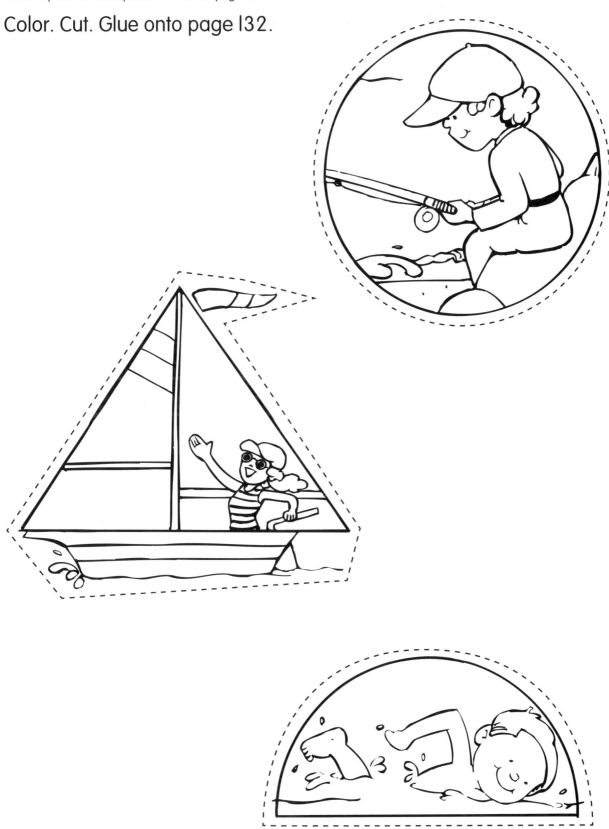

Name _____

How Many Fish?

Count the fish.

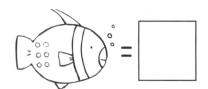 = ☐   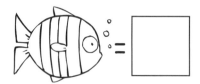 = ☐   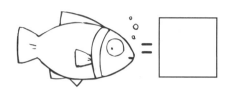 = ☐

How many fish in all?

Seasonal Activities • EMC 2002 • © Evan-Moor Corp.

Fishing

Color the fish. Count them.

How many fish in all?

Name _____

Draw the Fish

Make the fish in each box look the same.

Seasonal Activities • EMC 2002 • © Evan-Moor Corp.

Name _____

It Starts Like "Fish"

Color the pictures that start with the same sound as **fish**.

Trace the letters.

Name _____

A Picnic for Ant

Help Ant find his lunch.

Trace the letters.

yum

Seasonal Activities • EMC 2002 • © Evan-Moor Corp.

Name _____

The Picnic

Color the picture.

Count.

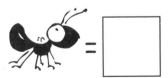 =

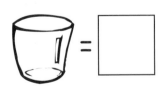 =

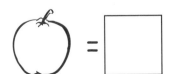 =

🍪 =

My Picnic Lunch

Pick the 4 foods you like best. Cut them out and glue them onto the picture.

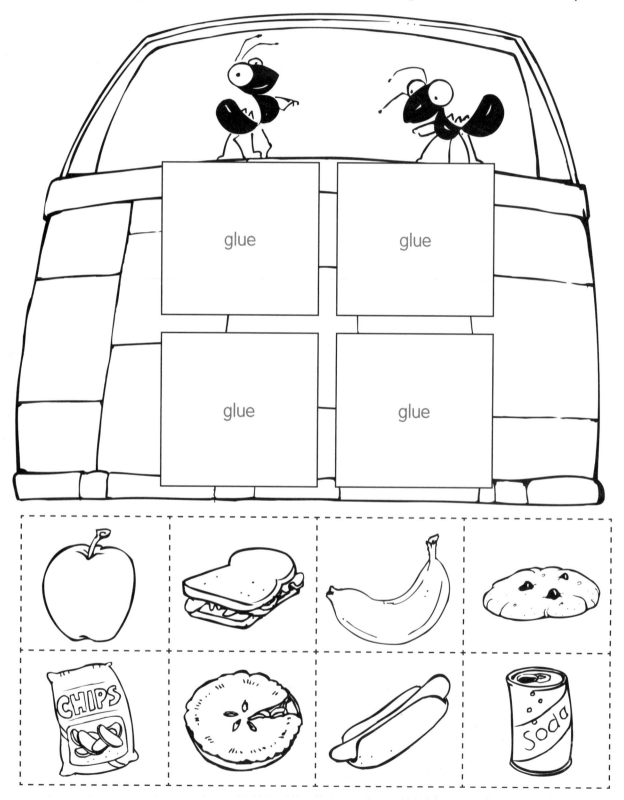

glue   glue

glue   glue

Seasonal Activities • EMC 2002 • © Evan-Moor Corp.

Name _____

My Vacation

Draw yourself on a vacation.

I went to _____
on vacation.

Name _____

My Father

Draw your father.

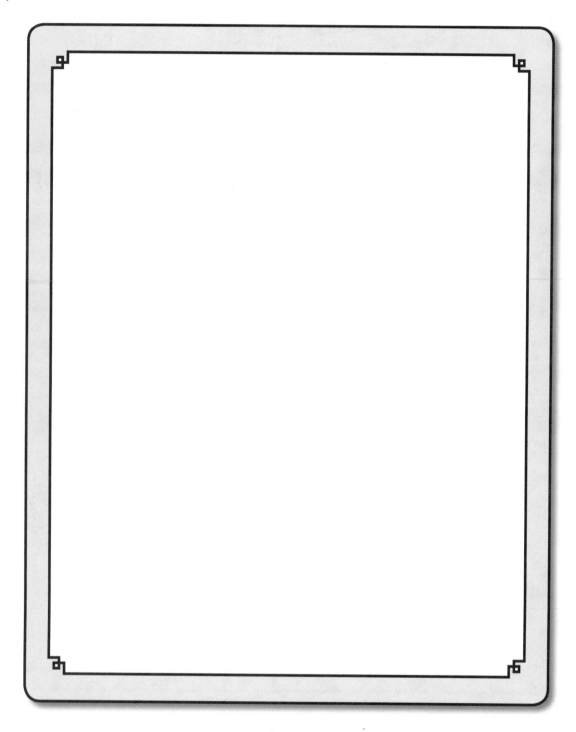

Trace.

Father

Name _____

Happy Father's Day

Color the picture. Trace the letters. Fold on the lines.

fold up

fold down

I love you, Dad!

A Parade

Cut out the puzzle. Glue the pieces inside the frame.

glue	glue
glue	glue

March in the parade on the 4th of July.

Seasonal Activities • EMC 2002 • © Evan-Moor Corp.

Our Flag

Color the flag parts on pages 146 & 147. Cut them out. Glue them together.

blue

Seasonal Activities • EMC 2002 • © Evan-Moor Corp.

I pledge allegiance to the flag of the United States of America.

glue

| red |
| white |
| red |
| white |
| red |
| white |
| red |
| white |
| red |
| white |
| red |
| white |
| red |

glue

Name _____

4th of July

Color the cake.

Trace the letters.

Happy Birthday, USA!

Seasonal Activities • EMC 2002 • © Evan-Moor Corp.

Answer Key

Autumn Page 7

Count the Leaves

Trace the numbers.
Color the leaves.

How many leaves?
10

Page 10

It Starts Like "Leaf"

Color the pictures that begin with the same sound as **leaf**.

leaf

Trace the letters.

Page 11

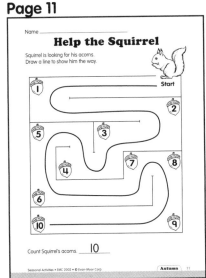

Help the Squirrel

Squirrel is looking for his acorns.
Draw a line to show him the way.

Start

Count Squirrel's acorns.   10

Page 12

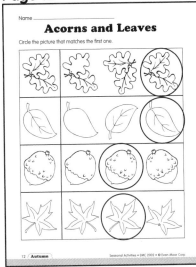

Acorns and Leaves

Circle the picture that matches the first one.

Page 13

In School

Color the classroom.

Count and write the numbers.

= 4   = 5   = 6
= 3   = 2   = 1

Page 14

School Tools

Color the tools you use at school.

Page 15

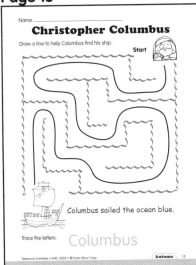

Christopher Columbus

Draw a line to help Columbus find his ship.

Start

Columbus sailed the ocean blue.

Trace the letters.

Columbus

Page 16

The *Santa Maria*

Color, cut, and glue to finish the ship.

Columbus sailed to America.
His ship was named the *Santa Maria*.

Page 18

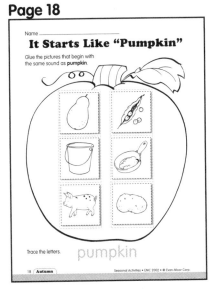

It Starts Like "Pumpkin"

Glue the pictures that begin with the same sound as **pumpkin**.

Trace the letters.

pumpkin

Page 20

Name _____

The Scarecrow

Cut out the puzzle. Glue the pieces inside the frame.

Trace the letters.

scarecrow

20 Autumn   Seasonal Activities • EMC 2002 • © Evan-Moor Corp.

Page 22

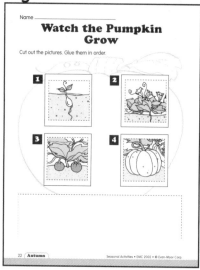

Name _____

Watch the Pumpkin Grow

Cut out the pictures. Glue them in order.

22 Autumn   Seasonal Activities • EMC 2002 • © Evan-Moor Corp.

Page 24

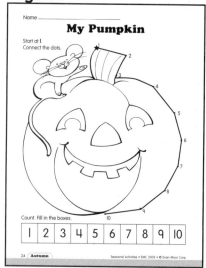

Name _____

My Pumpkin

Start at 1.
Connect the dots.

Count. Fill in the boxes.

| 1 | 2 | 3 | 4 | 5 | 6 | 7 | 8 | 9 | 10 |

24 Autumn   Seasonal Activities • EMC 2002 • © Evan-Moor Corp.

Page 25

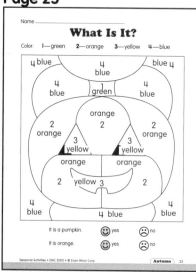

Name _____

What Is It?

Color: 1—green   2—orange   3—yellow   4—blue

It is a pumpkin.   ☺ yes   ☹ no
It is orange.   ☺ yes   ☹ no

Seasonal Activities • EMC 2002 • © Evan-Moor Corp.   Autumn 25

Page 27

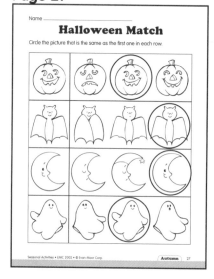

Name _____

Halloween Match

Circle the picture that is the same as the first one in each row.

Seasonal Activities • EMC 2002 • © Evan-Moor Corp.   Autumn 27

Page 28

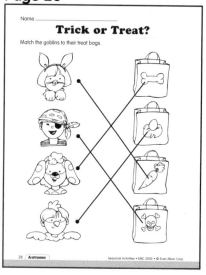

Name _____

Trick or Treat?

Match the goblins to their treat bags.

28 Autumn   Seasonal Activities • EMC 2002 • © Evan-Moor Corp.

Page 29

Name _____

Bat

Color, cut, and glue the ones that rhyme with **bat**.

Trace the letters.

bat

Seasonal Activities • EMC 2002 • © Evan-Moor Corp.   Autumn 29

Page 31

Name _____

The *Mayflower*

Connect the dots. Color the ship.

The Pilgrims came on the *Mayflower*.

Trace the letters.

Mayflower

Seasonal Activities • EMC 2002 • © Evan-Moor Corp.   Autumn 31

Page 32

Name _____

A Pilgrim Family

Color the Pilgrims. Cut and glue to finish the picture.

Father   Mother   Child

32 Autumn   Seasonal Activities • EMC 2002 • © Evan-Moor Corp.

Page 34

Page 36

Page 37

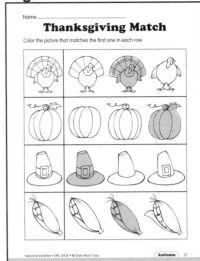

Page 38

Winter Page 46

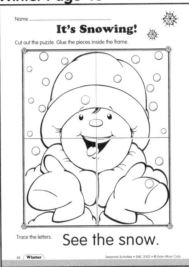

Page 48

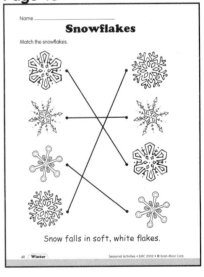

Page 50

Page 52

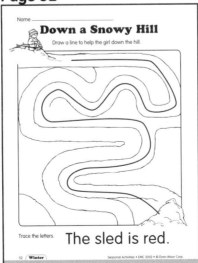

Page 53

Page 55

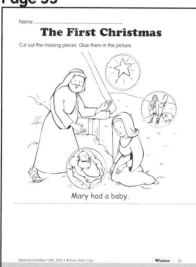

The First Christmas

Cut out the missing pieces. Glue them in the picture.

Mary had a baby.

Page 56

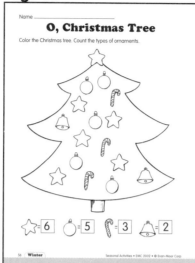

O, Christmas Tree

Color the Christmas tree. Count the types of ornaments.

⭐ = 6   🔴 = 5   🍬 = 3   🔔 = 2

Page 57

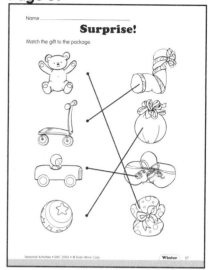

Surprise!

Match the gift to the package.

Page 58

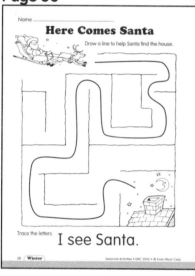

Here Comes Santa

Draw a line to help Santa find the house.

Trace the letters.

I see Santa.

Page 59

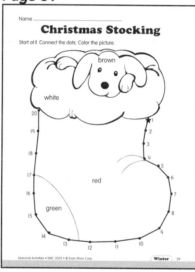

Christmas Stocking

Start at 1. Connect the dots. Color the picture.

brown
white
red
green

Page 60

Santa's Bag

Color Santa Claus. Draw a surprise in Santa's bag.

Pictures will vary.

Trace.

See the surprise.

Page 61

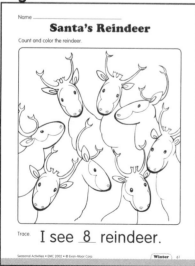

Santa's Reindeer

Count and color the reindeer.

Trace.

I see 8 reindeer.

Page 62

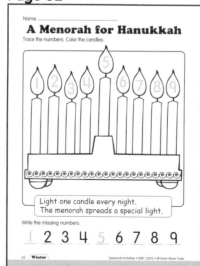

A Menorah for Hanukkah

Trace the numbers. Color the candles.

Light one candle every night.
The menorah spreads a special light.

Write the missing numbers.

1 2 3 4 5 6 7 8 9

Page 63

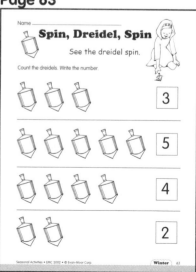

Spin, Dreidel, Spin

See the dreidel spin.

Count the dreidels. Write the number.

3

5

4

2

Page 65

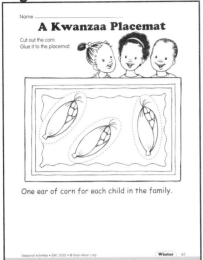

Name _____

A Kwanzaa Placemat

Cut out the corn.
Glue it to the placemat.

One ear of corn for each child in the family.

Page 66

Name _____

Happy New Year!

Connect the dots.
Trace and write the numbers for the year.

HAPPY
2 Answers
depend
on year

Page 68

Name _____

Martin Luther King, Jr.

Cut out the puzzle. Glue the pieces inside the frame.

He was a good man.
He was a brave man.
He was a fair man.

Page 72

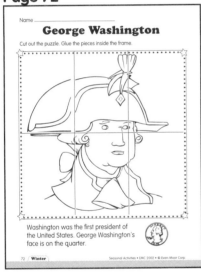

Name _____

George Washington

Cut out the puzzle. Glue the pieces inside the frame.

Washington was the first president of
the United States. George Washington's
face is on the quarter.

Page 74

Name _____

Abraham Lincoln

Cut out the puzzle. Glue the pieces inside the frame.

Lincoln was the 16th president of the
United States. Abraham Lincoln's face
is on the penny.

Page 76

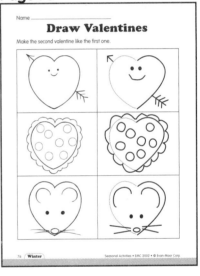

Name _____

Draw Valentines

Make the second valentine like the first one.

Page 77

Name _____

Hearts

Find the hearts. Color them.

Circle how many you found.

1 2 3 4 5 6 7 8 9 (10)

Page 78

Name _____

The Queen of Hearts

Color the tart red. Draw three more tarts.

red   red
red   red

The queen of hearts
Baked some tarts.

Page 79

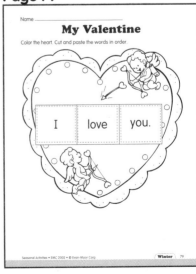

Name _____

My Valentine

Color the heart. Cut and paste the words in order.

I   love   you.

Spring Page 87

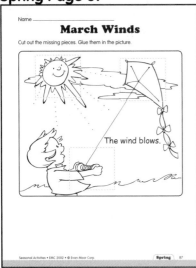

Page 88

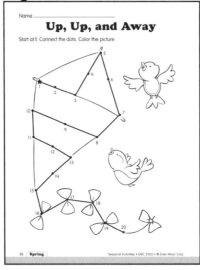

Page 89

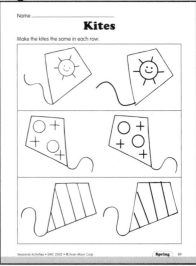

Page 90

Page 92

Page 94

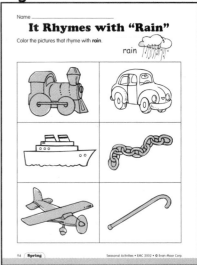

Page 95

Page 96

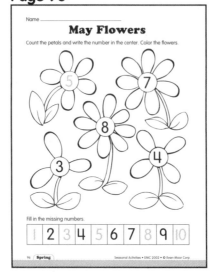

Page 97

Page 98

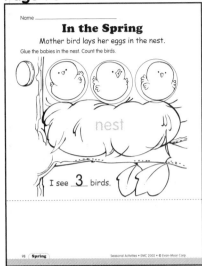

Name _____

In the Spring

Mother bird lays her eggs in the nest.

Glue the babies in the nest. Count the birds.

nest

I see __3__ birds.

98 Spring   Seasonal Activities • EMC 2002 • © Evan-Moor Corp.

Page 99

Name _____

A Butterfly Grows

Cut out the pictures. Glue them in order.

Fly away, butterfly!

1   **2**   **3**

Seasonal Activities • EMC 2002 • © Evan-Moor Corp.   Spring 99

Page 100

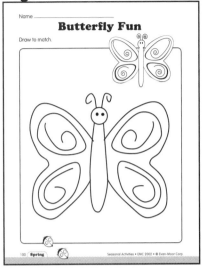

Name _____

Butterfly Fun

Draw to match.

100 Spring   Seasonal Activities • EMC 2002 • © Evan-Moor Corp.

Page 101

Name _____

Johnny Appleseed

Johnny Appleseed lived long ago.
He planted apple trees wherever he would go.

Find the apples. Color them.

I found __12__ apples.

Seasonal Activities • EMC 2002 • © Evan-Moor Corp.   Spring 101

Page 102

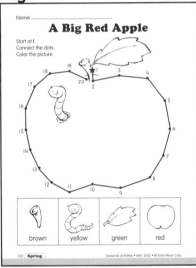

Name _____

A Big Red Apple

Start at 1.
Connect the dots.
Color the picture.

brown   yellow   green   red

102 Spring   Seasonal Activities • EMC 2002 • © Evan-Moor Corp.

Page 103

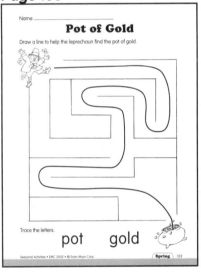

Name _____

Pot of Gold

Draw a line to help the leprechaun find the pot of gold.

Trace the letters.   pot   gold

Seasonal Activities • EMC 2002 • © Evan-Moor Corp.   Spring 103

Page 104

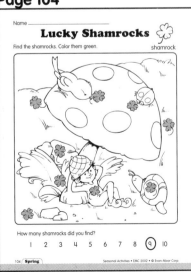

Name _____

Lucky Shamrocks

Find the shamrocks. Color them green.   shamrock

How many shamrocks did you find?

1   2   3   4   5   6   7   8   (9)   10

104 Spring   Seasonal Activities • EMC 2002 • © Evan-Moor Corp.

Page 105

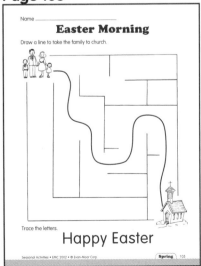

Name _____

Easter Morning

Draw a line to take the family to church.

Trace the letters.

Happy Easter

Seasonal Activities • EMC 2002 • © Evan-Moor Corp.   Spring 105

Page 106

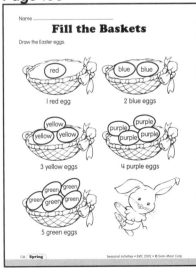

Name _____

Fill the Baskets

Draw the Easter eggs.

red   blue blue

1 red egg   2 blue eggs

yellow   purple purple
yellow yellow   purple purple

3 yellow eggs   4 purple eggs

green green
green green green

5 green eggs

106 Spring   Seasonal Activities • EMC 2002 • © Evan-Moor Corp.

Seasonal Activities • EMC 2002 • © Evan-Moor Corp.

Page 107

Page 108

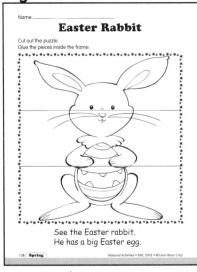

Page 110

Page 111

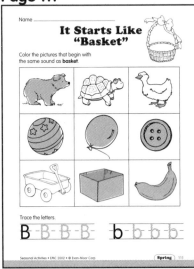

Page 112

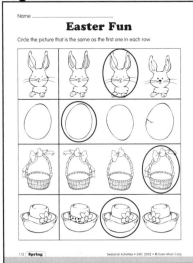

Page 113

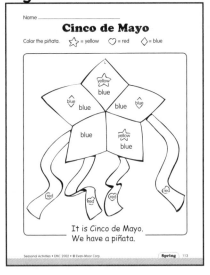

Page 114

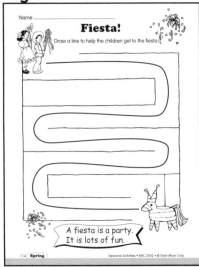

Page 116

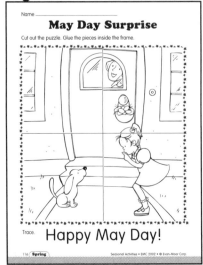

Page 119

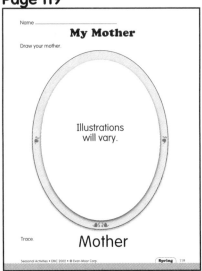

Summer Page 128

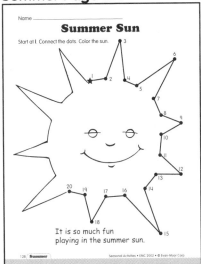

Summer Sun

Start at 1. Connect the dots. Color the sun.

It is so much fun
playing in the summer sun.

Page 130

Camping

Start at 1. Connect the dots.

It is fun to sleep in a tent.

Page 132

By the Sea

What fun
it will be
To play
by the sea.

Page 134

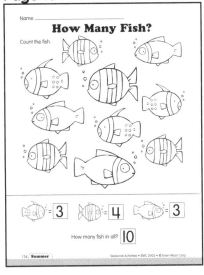

How Many Fish?

Count the fish.

= 3   = 4   = 3

How many fish in all? 10

Page 135

Fishing

Color the fish. Count them.

● = red   ▲ = orange   ■ = yellow

How many fish in all? 9

Page 136

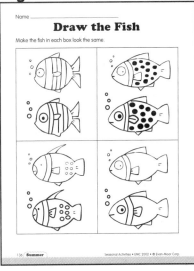

Draw the Fish

Make the fish in each box look the same.

Page 137

It Starts Like "Fish"

Color the pictures that start with the same sound as **fish**.

Trace the letters.

F

Page 138

A Picnic for Ant

Help Ant find his lunch.

Trace the letters.   yum

Page 139

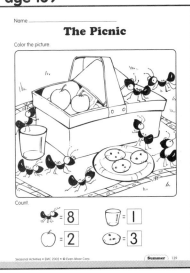

The Picnic

Color the picture.

Count.

= 8   = 1
= 2   = 3

Page 140

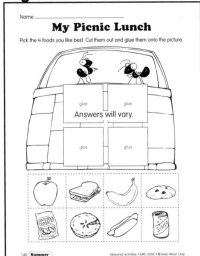

Page 142

Page 144

Notes

Notes

_____

_____

_____

_____

_____

_____

_____

_____

_____

_____

_____

_____

_____

_____

_____

_____